"Kids' Healthy Breakfast Recipes Book" is a cookbook designed especially for kids aged 3-12. It provides healthy and delicious recipes that are easy to make, with simple ingredients that can be found in any kitchen or grocery store. The book offers healthy breakfast recipes that are packed with nutrients and flavour, such as healthy pancakes, smoothies, and more. Each recipe includes an illustration to help children understand the instructions better, as well as nutritional information to help parents make healthy choices for their kids. The book also provides tips on healthy eating habits for young children and encourages them to try different recipes and healthy ingredients. With this book, kids can start their day with healthy delicious breakfast that will fuel them throughout the day.

Pancakes

This healthy breakfast recipe for kids is sure to become a family favorite! With only a few ingredients, it's easy to make and perfect for busy mornings. Start by mixing together 2 cups all-purpose flour, 2 teaspoons baking powder, ¼ teaspoon salt, and 1 tablespoon sugar (optional). Then add in the eggs and 1½ to 2 cups milk, and stir until the batter is smooth. Finally, add in 2 tablespoons melted and cooled butter (optional), or use a neutral oil for cooking. Heat up a skillet over medium-high heat and add butter or oil to coat the bottom of the pan. Drop about ¼ cup pancake batter into the pan per pancake. Cook until the edges begin to look golden and bubbles appear on the top of each pancake. Flip the pancakes over, cook for another minute or two, then remove from heat and serve with your favorite toppings! Enjoy!

This healthy breakfast recipe for kids is not only easy to make but also incredibly delicious. Kids will love the fluffy pancakes and parents will love the healthy ingredients. The best part is that everyone can have breakfast ready in no time! With this healthy breakfast recipe for kids, you've got a surefire way to start your mornings off right.

Enjoy!

Oatmeal

Oatmeal is a healthy breakfast recipe for kids that is easy to make. All you need are 4 simple ingredients: old fashioned oats or rolled oats, milk, water and a little salt. With these four basic ingredients, you can start your day off with a healthy and delicious bowl of oatmeal.

Oats provide essential vitamins and minerals and are a great source of healthy carbohydrates. Combined with milk and water, oatmeal is a nutritious breakfast option that can help fuel your little ones for the day ahead. All you need to do is mix the oats, milk, water and salt together in a pot on the stove or in a bowl in the microwave. Cook until it reaches your desired consistency and you're ready to enjoy a healthy breakfast.

Adding your favorite toppings like fruit, nuts, cinnamon and honey can also add extra flavor and nutrition to your oatmeal bowl. Oatmeal is an easy and healthy breakfast option for kids of all ages that won't take long to make in the morning. Start your day off with this healthy breakfast recipe for kids that's sure to please everyone!

This healthy breakfast recipe for kids is sure to become a regular part of your morning routine with its few ingredients and fast prep time. Get creative in the kitchen by adding different flavors or mix-ins – there are endless possibilities when it comes to making a healthy bowl of oatmeal! Try out this healthy breakfast recipe for kids today to kickstart healthy habits for your family.

Happy cooking!

Fruit and Nut Bars

INGREDIENTS:
1 c. pitted dates (about 12)
1/4 c. peanut or almond butter
1/4 c. honey
1 tsp. pure vanilla extract
1 c. roasted unsalted almonds, roughly chopped
1/2 c. rolled oats
3/4 c. dried fruit (cranberries, golden raisins, sliced apricots)
1/4 c. pumpkin seeds

Fruit and Nut Bars are a delicious and healthy snack for kids! They are easy to make and full of nutritious ingredients like dates, peanut or almond butter, honey, vanilla extract, almonds, oats, dried fruit, and pumpkin seeds. Not only are these bars packed with superfoods but they also provide plenty of energy-boosting nutrients and fiber. Plus, they only take a few minutes to make and can be enjoyed as an on-the-go snack or after school treat! Make a batch of these bars today and give your kids a healthy snack that they will love.

Enjoying healthy foods doesn't have to be boring or difficult. These Fruit and Nut Bars are a fun and tasty way to get the nutritional benefits of dates, nuts, oats, dried fruit, and pumpkin seeds. Plus, they're so easy to make that anyone can do it! Just mix all the ingredients together in a bowl and then form into bars or small balls. Then you can wrap them up for an easy snack to take on the go or store in an airtight container in the refrigerator. With healthy recipes like this, your kids are sure to stay full and energized all day long!

Making healthy snacks for your family doesn't have to be hard or boring. With simple ingredients like those found in these Fruit and Nut Bars, you can whip up a healthy snack that your kids will love. Try it today and enjoy the benefits of healthy ingredients like dates, nuts, oats, dried fruit, and pumpkin seeds!

Happy snacking!

Love Toast

INGREDIENTS:
- ¼ tsp. mayonnaise
- 2 slice white sandwich bread
- 1 tbsp. butter
- 2 large eggs
- salt
- Pepper
- Finely chopped capers
- Finely chopped fresh herbs

Love Toast is a healthy, delicious meal that can be enjoyed by children and adults alike! This recipe takes just minutes to prepare, making it an ideal meal for busy families. The ingredients are simple but flavorful – mayonnaise, white sandwich bread, butter, eggs, salt, pepper, capers and fresh herbs. Together they create a tasty, healthy sandwich that kids will love!

To make Love Toast, start by toasting the bread in a skillet over medium heat. Spread each slice with mayonnaise and set aside. Next, melt butter in the same skillet and crack two eggs into it. Cook until the whites are set but the yolks are still runny. Place the eggs on top of the mayonnaise-covered bread slices. Sprinkle with a bit of salt and pepper, then top with capers and fresh herbs. Serve warm and enjoy!

Love Toast is a healthy recipe for kids that is simple to make, full of flavor, and sure to be a hit. With its great taste and easy-to-follow instructions, this healthy meal is sure to become a regular in your family's rotation. Try Love Toast today and see for yourself why it's such a crowd-pleaser!

Banana Cream Oats

INGREDIENTS:
1 ripe banana, peeled
1/2 c. low-fat cottage cheese (preferably whipped)
1/4 c. unsweetened almond milk (or milk of choice)
1/4 c. old-fashioned oats
1 tbsp. chia seeds
1 tsp. pure vanilla extract
OPTIONAL TOPPERS: Sliced bananas, toasted walnuts, shredded unsweetened coconut, and/or ground cinnamon

Banana Cream Oats is a healthy, delicious breakfast option that kids will love. This recipe has only five simple ingredients: one ripe banana, 1/2 cup low-fat cottage cheese (preferably whipped), 1/4 cup unsweetened almond milk (or other milk of choice), 1/4 cup old-fashioned oats, 1 tablespoon of chia seeds, and 1 teaspoon of pure vanilla extract. The healthy oats will give your kids all the energy they need to get through their day.

To make this healthy recipe even more delicious, you can add toppings like sliced bananas, toasted walnuts, shredded unsweetened coconut and/or ground cinnamon. Your kids will love the healthy breakfast treat and you can feel good knowing that it's a nutritious meal to start their day. Banana Cream Oats is just one of many healthy recipes for kids you can make in minutes.
Enjoy!

Biscuits with Bacon, Cheddar, and Chives

These healthy Biscuits with Bacon, Cheddar, and Chives, are a great way to get your kids eating healthy. The recipe is made with nutritious ingredients like cauliflower florets or "rice", blanched almond flour, baking powder and reduced-fat sharp cheddar cheese. It also includes egg whites for protein, and healthy fat sources like butter and turkey bacon. To give it some flavor, you can also add chives to the mix. These biscuits are sure to be a hit with your kids! Plus, they won't even know that these healthy treats contain healthy ingredients. So get creative and try out this healthy recipe for your family today!

The ingredients you'll need to make this healthy biscuit recipe are: 4 c. cauliflower florets (or 3 cups cauliflower "rice"), 1/2 c. blanched almond flour, 1 tsp. baking powder, 1/2 tsp. kosher salt, 1/2 c. shredded 2% reduced-fat sharp Cheddar cheese, 2 large egg whites, lightly beaten, 2 tbsp. unsalted butter, melted, 3 to 4 strips turkey bacon, cooked and crumbled, and 2 tbsp. chopped fresh chives.

Once you've gathered the ingredients together it's time to get started! Preheat your oven to 375°F and line a baking sheet with parchment paper. In a large bowl, combine the cauliflower florets or "rice", almond flour, baking powder, salt and cheese. Stir in the egg whites and melted butter until everything is evenly combined. Then fold in the bacon and chives.

Using your hands, shape the dough into round biscuits and place on the parchment-lined baking sheet. Bake for 20 minutes or until golden brown. Allow to cool before serving.

These healthy Biscuits with Bacon, Cheddar, and Chives are sure to be a hit with your kids! They're full of healthy ingredients that you can feel good about feeding your family. Plus, they're delicious and easy to make! Give this healthy recipe a try today and watch as your kids devour every last bite. Enjoy!

Raspberry Smoothie Bowl

INGREDIENTS:
2 c. frozen raspberries
2 bananas
1/2 c. nonfat Greek yogurt
1 tbsp. chia seeds (optional)
1/2 c. low fat milk
Granola, for serving
Toasted coconut flakes, for serving

This healthy Raspberry Smoothie Bowl is the perfect recipe for kids and adults alike! It's loaded with healthy ingredients like frozen raspberries, bananas, nonfat Greek yogurt, chia seeds (optional), low fat milk, granola and toasted coconut flakes. All you need to do is blend all the ingredients together for a delicious smoothie bowl that is healthy and packed with vitamins, minerals and fiber. To add an extra healthy touch, you can also top your smoothie bowl with fresh fruit or a sprinkle of nuts for added flavor and crunch. This healthy Raspberry Smoothie Bowl is sure to be a hit with both kids and adults! Enjoy!

Peanut Butter and Jelly Muffins

INGREDIENTS:
- 1 c. wheat bran
- 1 c. whole-wheat flour
- 1/2 c. granulated sugar
- 1 tsp. baking powder
- 1/2 tsp. baking soda
- 1/2 tsp. ground cinnamon
- 1 pinch kosher salt
- 1/4 c. unsweetened applesauce
- 1/2 c. buttermilk
- 1/4 c. olive oil
- 1 large egg
- 1 c. small red grapes
- 10 tsp. creamy peanut butter
- 1 tbsp. water
- 1/4 c. seedless jam

Are you looking for healthy recipes to make with your kids? Look no further than these delicious peanut butter and jelly muffins! Not only are they easy to make, but they're also a healthy alternative to traditional sugary desserts.

These muffins have an array of healthy ingredients such as wheat bran, whole-wheat flour, applesauce, buttermilk and olive oil. They also include a healthy dose of cinnamon and some delicious 10 teaspoons of creamy peanut butter!

To complete the recipe, you'll need to mix together 1 cup of small red grapes with 1 tablespoon of water and ¼ cup seedless jam. This mixture will be swirled throughout the muffin batter to create a delightful jammy surprise.

When all the ingredients are combined and baked, they make healthy and delicious muffins that your kids will love. Enjoy!

Hope you have fun making these healthy peanut butter and jelly muffins with your kids! They're sure to enjoy them as much as you do.

Happy baking!

Herb Omelette with Tomatoes

Ingredients:

1 tsp olive oil
3 tomatoes, halved
4 large eggs
1 tbsp chopped parsley
1 tbsp chopped basil

Herb omelette with tomatoes is a healthy and delicious meal that can easily be made for kids. Start by heating the olive oil in a pan over medium heat. Once warm, add the tomatoes and cook until they are softened and slightly browned. In a bowl, whisk together the eggs, parsley, and basil until combined. Pour the egg mixture into the pan over the tomatoes. Swirl around to evenly distribute it in the pan. Cook until golden on one side and then flip over to finish cooking on the other side for about two minutes or until cooked through. Serve warm with a sprinkle of chopped herbs or healthy sides of your choice. This easy-to-make meal is sure to please even picky eaters! With its healthy and delicious ingredients, this herb omelette with tomatoes is an excellent healthy recipe for kids.
Enjoy!

Banana Smoothie

To make this banana smoothie, you'll need two small bananas (or one large), 1 cup of ice cubes, 3/4 cup unsweetened almond milk, 1/4 cup plain yogurt, 1 tablespoon of flaxseed and 2 teaspoons of honey. To make the smoothie, simply place all of the ingredients in a blender and blend until everything is combined. Serve immediately and enjoy!

This healthy banana smoothie is sure to be a hit with both kids and adults alike. With its nutritious ingredients, it's perfect for adding some healthy sweetness to your family's mealtime routine. So go ahead and give this healthy banana smoothie a try today! Your kids will thank you.

To give your banana smoothie an extra healthy boost, you can also add a spoonful of chia seeds or some fresh berries. This healthy recipe is so versatile and sure to become a favorite with your family in no time. Enjoy!

Avocado Smoothie

Avocado smoothie is a healthy and delicious snack that can be easily made at home. It's perfect for kids who want something healthy and tasty to munch on in between meals. To make an avocado smoothie, you will need unsweetened almond milk, ice, half an avocado, maple syrup, and chia seeds. First, blend the almond milk, ice, and avocado together in a blender until smooth. Then add the maple syrup and chia seeds and blend for another few seconds. Serve immediately or store in an airtight container in the refrigerator for up to two days. This healthy snack is packed with healthy fats from the avocado and fiber from the chia seeds, making it a perfect healthy snack for kids.
Enjoy!

Mango Smoothie

Ingredients:
1 c. frozen mango
1 c. coconut water
1/2 c. plain yogurt
1 small banana
1 tsp. honey (optional)
1/8 tsp. ground nutmeg

This healthy Mango Smoothie is a quick and easy recipe that kids of all ages will love. With only five ingredients, this smoothie is simple enough for even the smallest helpers to make! It's packed with vitamins and minerals from frozen mango, coconut water, plain yogurt, banana, and a hint of honey (optional) and nutmeg. It's sure to please even the pickiest of eaters, making it a healthy and delicious treat that your kids will love. So, why not whip up this Mango Smoothie for a refreshing snack or healthy lunch that your little ones can enjoy!

This recipe is perfect for busy families who are looking for healthy recipes for kids. Smoothies are a great way to get in lots of vitamins and minerals, as well as the added bonus of convenience. This Mango Smoothie is healthy enough to enjoy on-the-go or at home and sure to become a family favorite! So grab your ingredients, grab your blender and make this healthy and delicious Mango Smoothie today! Enjoy!

French Toast

Ingredients

1 (1-lb.) loaf cinnamon twist or plain brioche, cut into 1"-thick slices
4 large eggs
1 c. whole milk
1/2 c. heavy cream
2 tbsp. granulated sugar
1 tsp. ground cinnamon
1 tsp. pure vanilla extract
1/4 tsp. ground nutmeg
Kosher salt
3 tbsp. unsalted butter, divided, plus more if needed
Maple syrup, mixed berries, and confectioners' sugar, for serving
(optional)

This healthy French toast recipe is a great breakfast option for kids and adults alike! Featuring an array of healthy, nutritious ingredients such as eggs, whole milk, heavy cream, cinnamon and nutmeg, this French toast is sure to be a hit with the whole family. It's also incredibly easy to make - just whisk together the eggs, milk, cream, sugar, cinnamon and nutmeg in a large bowl. Dip the brioche slices into the egg mixture and fry them in a skillet with 2 tablespoons of butter. Serve the French toast with healthy toppings such as berries, maple syrup and a sprinkle of confectioners' sugar. With healthy recipes like this one, kids can start the day with a delicious, nutritious breakfast.

Enjoy!

Buttermilk Pancakes

Ingredients
2 c. all-purpose flour
2 1/2 tbsp. granulated sugar
1 tsp. baking powder
1 tsp. baking osda
1 tsp. kosher salt
2 1/2 c. buttermilk
2 eggs, separated
4 tbsp. unsalted butter, melted, plus more for serving
Vegetable oil, for cooking
Maple syrup, for serving

These healthy buttermilk pancakes are the perfect choice for a delicious, nutritious breakfast. Not only are they full of healthy ingredients like all-purpose flour, granulated sugar, baking powder and baking soda, kosher salt, buttermilk, eggs, butter, and vegetable oil - they're also incredibly simple to make. With only a few steps and limited ingredients, kids can easily help make this healthy recipe.

To begin, whisk together the all-purpose flour, sugar, baking powder, baking soda and salt in a large bowl. In a separate bowl, whisk together the buttermilk and egg yolks until combined. Make sure to save the whites for later! Pour the buttermilk mixture into the flour mixture and stir until combined. Then add in the melted butter and mix until everything is smooth.

In a separate bowl, beat the egg whites with a hand mixer or whisk until stiff peaks form. Gently fold them into the batter using a spatula. Heat a large skillet over medium heat and brush with vegetable oil.

Using a 1/4 cup measuring cup, scoop the batter into the skillet and cook until golden brown on both sides. Serve with extra butter, maple syrup, or your favorite topping. This healthy recipe for kids is sure to be a hit! Enjoy!

Puff Pastry Hot Dogs

Ingredients
1 (8-oz.) can Crescent dough
3 slices American cheese
12 hot dogs
2 tbsp. melted butter
Dijon mustard

Puff Pastry Hot Dogs make a healthy, fun meal for kids that can be cooked in no time. All you need is Crescent dough, American cheese slices, hot dogs, melted butter and Dijon mustard for the perfect Halloween-themed dinner. Start by preheating your oven to 375°F. Separate the crescent dough into triangles and place each triangle onto a baking sheet. Cut cheese slices into thin strips and wrap them around the hot dogs to create mummies, making sure that all sides of the hot dog are covered with cheese. Place each mummy on top of a crescent triangle and fold up the corners to cover the hot dog. Brush melted butter over the dough and bake for 12-14 minutes. When finished, use Dijon mustard to create eyes for the mummies and serve.

Mummy Hot Dogs are a great healthy option to serve as an alternative to traditional sugary snacks during the holiday season. Kids will love being able to make and customize their own mummies to enjoy. This easy-to-make recipe takes no time and is sure to be a hit with your children.

Enjoy !

Overnight Oats

Overnight oats are a healthy and delicious breakfast option that will keep you feeling full until lunch. With just a few basic ingredients – oats, chia seeds, cocoa powder, almond milk, peanut butter, banana, salt and vanilla extract – you can have delicious overnight oats ready for the morning. Simply mix all of the ingredients together in a jar the night before and leave in the fridge overnight. In the morning, you'll have healthy and filling oats that are ready to eat. Top with a few slices of banana for extra flavor and sweetness or any other topping of your choice for a delicious start to the day! Enjoy!

Bacon and Egg Cups

Bacon and Egg Cups are a healthy and delicious breakfast option for kids. They only require a few simple ingredients, including 12 slices of whole wheat bread, 12 large eggs, 3/4 cup of shredded Cheddar cheese, 4 slices of precooked bacon, salt and freshly ground pepper to taste, and chopped chives for garnish. The egg and bacon cups can be baked in a muffin tin, making them the perfect grab-and-go breakfast for busy mornings. Not only are they healthy and delicious, but they are also easy to make and store for up to four days in the refrigerator. Kids will love the tasty combination of eggs, cheese, bacon, and bread – it's sure to keep them energized and ready for the day ahead. So why not whip up a batch of these healthy Bacon and Egg Cups to make morning meal time more exciting?

You can even get creative by adding vegetables like mushrooms, bell peppers, or spinach for an extra healthy kick. The possibilities are endless! So go ahead and make breakfast time a healthy and happy affair with these tasty Bacon and Egg Cups. Kids will love them!

Happy cooking!

Grain Bowl

INGREDIENTS
1 tbsp. olive oil, plus more for drizzling
1 clove garlic, finely chopped
1 bunch spinach, roughly chopped
kosher salt
black pepper
2 c. leftover cooked grains (brown rice, quinoa, or couscous)
1/2 avocado, roughly chopped
1 tomato, cut into 1" pieces

Grain Bowls are a healthy and delicious breakfast option for kids that can be easily customized to their tastes. Start by warming the olive oil in a pan over medium heat. Add garlic and spinach, season with salt and pepper, and sauté until the spinach is wilted. Add in cooked grains of your choice, such as brown rice, quinoa, or couscous and cook until warmed through. Transfer to a bowl and top with chopped avocado and tomato pieces. Drizzle with olive oil for extra flavor and healthy fats. Grain Bowls can be made ahead of time and stored in the fridge as healthy grab-and-go breakfasts for busy mornings.

Enjoy!

Egg Sandwich

INGREDIENTS
2 large eggs
1 tbsp. finely chopped dill
1 tbsp. finely chopped chives
kosher salt
black pepper
2 English muffins, toasted
2 slices Cheddar
1 plum tomato, sliced

Egg sandwiches are a healthy and delicious breakfast that your kids will love! Start with the ingredients mentioned above, or you can mix it up with your own favorites. Crack two eggs into a bowl and whisk together with dill, chives, salt, and pepper. Heat a skillet over medium heat and pour in egg mixture. As the eggs cook, stir them with a spatula to break up into small pieces. When the eggs are fully cooked, rcmove from heat. Toast two English muffins and top each one with a slice of cheese. Place a spoonful of egg salad onto each muffin and top with tomato slices. Now you have a healthy breakfast for kids that's full of flavor and nutrition! Happy cooking!

Mozzarella Avocado Toast

Ingredients
1 avocado
1/2 Juice of 1/2 lemon
Kosher salt
Freshly ground black pepper
2 thick slices sourdough, toasted
1/2 c. halved cherry tomatoes
1 c. mozzarella balls (such as Ciliegine)
Flaky sea salt
2 freshly sliced basil leaves
Balsamic glaze, for drizzling

Mozzarella Avocado Toast is a healthy and delicious breakfast option for kids. This easy-to-make dish only requires a few simple ingredients, making it an ideal choice for busy mornings. To prepare this recipe, start by toasting two thick slices of sourdough in your oven or toaster. In the meantime, mash one avocado and mix it with the juice of half a lemon, as well as some kosher salt and freshly ground black pepper. Spread the avocado mixture onto each piece of toast generously. Then top with halved cherry tomatoes, mozzarella balls, flaky sea salt, and freshly sliced basil leaves. Finally, drizzle with balsamic glaze for an added layer of flavor. This healthy breakfast for kids is sure to bring a smile to their faces and fuel them up for a busy day ahead!
Enjoy!

Chia Pudding

Ingredients
CHIA SEEDS ,MILK, SWEETENER ,VANILLA ,COCOA POWDER ,NUT OR SEED BUTTER ,FRUIT

Chia pudding is a healthy and delicious breakfast option for kids. It's packed with healthy nutrients such as protein, dietary fiber, healthy fats, and essential minerals like calcium, iron, magnesium, and zinc. Chia pudding can be made in minutes using just a few simple ingredients including chia seeds, milk or plant-based milk of your choice, sweetener such as honey or maple syrup, and a touch of vanilla. To make it even more special, top it off with cocoa powder and nut butter for extra protein and healthy fats. Add your favorite fruit to complete this healthy breakfast that's sure to please the whole family! With chia pudding you can be confident that your kids are getting the healthy fuel they need to power through the day.

Enjoy!

Scrambled Eggs

Ingredients
Eggs
Milk, plant milk, or water
Extra-virgin olive oil or butter
Salt...
And pepper!

Scrambled eggs are a healthy and quick breakfast option for kids. With just a few simple ingredients--eggs, milk, plant milk, water, extra-virgin olive oil or butter, salt and pepper--you can whip up a healthy meal in minutes! Start by cracking the eggs into a bowl and adding your choice of liquid (dairy, plant-based, or water). Whisk everything together until fully blended. Heat some butter or extra-virgin olive oil in a skillet and pour the egg mixture in. Move the eggs around with a spatula as they cook and season with salt and pepper to taste. When the eggs are lightly golden and fluffy, they're ready to serve. Scrambled eggs are a healthy and delicious breakfast option for kids that can be served with toast, fresh fruit, or a smoothie. With its simple ingredients and straightforward preparation, scrambled eggs are the perfect healthy breakfast for busy mornings!
Happy cooking!

Classic French Crepes

Ingredients: for
1 ¼ cup milk 10 fl oz.
3 large eggs.
2 tbsp oil or melted butter.
2 tsp sugar for savory crepes, OR.
3 tbsp sugar for sweet dessert crepes.
½ tsp kosher salt.
4 oz all purpose flour scant 1 cup.
fruits

Classic French Crepes are a healthy breakfast option for kids. They are easy to make with just a few simple ingredients such as milk, eggs, oil or melted butter, sugar, salt and all-purpose flour. With this recipe you can choose to make savory or sweet crepes depending on your preference. Simply mix all of the ingredients together in a large bowl, heat up a crepe pan or griddle, and then cook the crepes for about 2 minutes on each side. Serve with your favorite toppings such as jam, honey, fruits or chocolate. Your kids will love these healthy and delicious French Crepes for breakfast!

Enjoy!

Strawberry Muffins

Ingredients

½ cup milk
¼ cup canola oil
1 large egg
1 ¾ cups all-purpose flour
½ cup white sugar
2 teaspoons baking powder
½ teaspoon salt
1 cup chopped strawberries

Strawberry Muffins are a great healthy breakfast for kids. Not only are they delicious, but they're also easy to make using simple ingredients. All you need is milk, canola oil, an egg, all-purpose flour, sugar, baking powder and salt. Once you have these basic ingredients, the rest is just about adding your favorite fruits, like strawberries. Simply chop the strawberries and mix them into the batter for a tasty treat that your kids will love. Serve up these muffins with a glass of cold milk or juice and you've got a delicious breakfast! Healthy, easy and delicious - what more could you ask for? Your kids are sure to love these Strawberry Muffins.

Enjoy!

Pumpkin Oatmeal Cookies

Ingredients
- 2 Cup(s) flour, all-purpose
- 1 1/3 Cup(s) Quaker® Oats (quick or old fashioned)
- 1 Teaspoon(s) Baking Soda
- 1 Teaspoon(s) Cinnamon
- 1/2 Teaspoon(s) Salt
- 1 Cup(s) butter or margarine, softened
- 1 Cup(s) Sugar
- 1 Cup(s) Brown sugar, packed
- 1 Cup(s) canned pumpkin {NOT pumpkin pie filling}
- 1 Teaspoon(s) vanilla
- 3/4 Cup(s) Chopped Walnuts
- 3/4 Cup(s) raisins
- 1 Egg(s)

These delicious Pumpkin Oatmeal Cookies are the perfect way to give your kids a healthy start to their day. Packed full of nutritious ingredients like all-purpose flour, Quaker® Oats, baking soda, cinnamon, salt, butter or margarine, sugar, brown sugar, canned pumpkin (not pumpkin pie filling), vanilla extract, chopped walnuts, raisins, and one egg, these treats will provide a boost of energy to kick off their day. Plus, they're sure to love the sweet pumpkin flavor! Enjoy a warm batch of these cookies for breakfast and feel good about giving your kids a healthy start. Enjoy!

Banana Split Bowl

Ingredients
1 1/4 cups Kellogg's® Rice Krispies® cereal.
1/3 cup quartered strawberries.
1/4 small banana, split lengthwise and sliced.
2 teaspoons chocolate syrup (optional)
2 tablespoons frozen non-dairy whipped topping, thawed, or aerosol whipped cream.
1/2 teaspoon rainbow sprinkles.
1/2 cup fat-free milk.

This delicious and easy-to-make breakfast bowl is a great way to add fun to your kids' morning routine! The Breakfast Banana Split Bowl contains Kellogg's® Rice Krispies® cereal, strawberries, banana slices, chocolate syrup (optional), non-dairy whipped topping or aerosol cream, sprinkles, and fat-free milk. The combination of these ingredients makes a tasty and nutritious breakfast that your kids will love!

This dish can be made the night before so it's ready in the morning. Simply mix together Rice Krispies® cereal, quartered strawberries, sliced banana slices, chocolate syrup (optional), non-dairy whipped topping or aerosol cream, and rainbow sprinkles. Then add fat-free milk to your desired consistency. Refrigerate overnight so the flavors can meld and enjoy in the morning! Enjoy!

Banana and Peanut Butter

INGREDIENTS

4 lightly salted brown rice cakes
2 bananas
¼ cup peanut butter sub sunflower butter if allergic to peanuts

Tired of the same old breakfast ideas for kids? Try this creative and healthy alternative! Banana and Peanut Butter Rice Cakes are a great way to start your day. All you need is four lightly salted brown rice cakes, two ripe bananas, and ¼ cup of peanut butter (substitute sunflower butter if there is an allergy to peanuts). Spread the peanut butter over each rice cake, then slice the bananas and layer them on top. Serve and enjoy! This quick and simple breakfast idea for kids is sure to put a smile on their faces.

Bon Appetit!

Carrot Cake Pancakes

INGREDIENTS
- all purpose flour (can sub whole wheat)
- brown sugar
- baking powder
- cozy spices like cinnamon, nutmeg and ginger
- carrots
- chopped walnuts
- egg
- milk
- butter
- vanilla extract
- maple syrup and coconut flakes (optional for topping)

Carrot Cake Pancakes are the perfect breakfast idea to get kids excited about mornings! Made with all-natural ingredients like flour, brown sugar, baking powder, cozy spices like cinnamon, nutmeg and ginger, carrots, chopped walnuts, eggs, milk, butter and vanilla extract.

These pancakes are an easy way to sneak in some veggies and are sure to be a hit with kids.

Top them off with some maple syrup and coconut flakes as an optional treat, and enjoy this delicious breakfast! Kids will love the sweet taste of these carrot cake pancakes while still getting all the nutrition they need in the morning. Start their day off right with this healthy and tasty breakfast!
Enjoy!

Burrito Breakfast

Ingredients
1 lb. seasoned ground pork sausage ✓
8 large eggs, whisked
1 cup diced peppers
3/4 cup shredded sharp cheddar cheese ✓
8 large gluten-free flour tortillas
1 tbsp. olive oil

Looking for a breakfast idea the kids will love? Try this delicious burrito breakfast!

Start by browning the ground pork sausage in a skillet with 1 tablespoon of olive oil over medium heat. Once cooked through, add in the diced peppers and cook until soft.

Next, whisk together 8 large eggs and pour them into the skillet. Use a spoon to stir and scramble the eggs with the sausage and peppers.

Once the eggs are fully cooked, turn off the heat and stir in 3/4 cup of shredded sharp cheddar cheese.

Warm up 8 large gluten-free flour tortillas in a separate skillet or in a warm oven.

Fill each tortilla with the egg, sausage and pepper mixture.

Voila! A delicious burrito breakfast the kids are sure to love.

For an extra kick of flavor, add a teaspoon of your favorite hot sauce or salsa. Enjoy!

Blueberry Smoothie With Cottage Cheese

Ingredients
1 cup spinach
2/3 cup blueberries
1/2 large overripe frozen banana
1/2 cup almond milk or milk of choice
2 teaspoons maple syrup ✓
3/4 cup cottage cheese ✓

Blueberry smoothie with cottage cheese is a delicious and nutritious breakfast idea for kids. It's packed full of vitamins and minerals, providing essential nutrients to keep your child going throughout the day. This smoothie is simple to make, requiring only 6 ingredients: spinach, blueberries, an overripe frozen banana, almond milk or other milk of choice, maple syrup, and cottage cheese. Spinach helps to provide a healthy dose of vitamins A and K, while the blueberries offer antioxidants. The frozen banana adds natural sweetness and creaminess, and the almond milk ensures smooth consistency. Maple syrup helps to sweeten the smoothie without adding too much sugar, while the cottage cheese adds a healthy dose of protein and calcium. With these 6 simple ingredients, you can whip up this delicious breakfast in no time! Kids will love the sweet, creamy taste – and parents can rest assured that they're giving their children a nutritious start to the day. Enjoy!

Banana Muffins

Banana muffins are the perfect breakfast idea for kids! Not only do they taste delicious, but they are also healthy and easy to make.

Start by preheating the oven to 375°F. In a large bowl, combine 3/4 cup brown sugar, 1/2 cup granulated sugar, 2 large eggs, 2 teaspoons of almond extract, 1 cup Greek yogurt, and 4 over-ripe mashed bananas.

In a separate bowl, mix together 3 1/2 cups gluten-free all-purpose flour, 1/4 cup ground flax seed, 1 teaspoon baking soda, and 1 teaspoon salt. Add the dry ingredients to the wet ingredients and mix until combined. Stir in 1 cup chocolate chips.

Divide the batter evenly among a muffin tin lined with paper liners, filling each cup about 3/4 of the way full. Bake for 18-20 minutes or until a toothpick inserted in the center comes out clean. Allow to cool for 5-10 minutes before serving. Enjoy these delicious banana muffins with your kids! Enjoy!

I want to take a moment to express my heartfelt gratitude for your recent purchase of my recipe book. As a passionate food lover, nothing makes me happier than sharing my favorite recipes with others. Your decision to invest in my book not only supports my dream, but also shows your commitment to expanding your culinary horizons.

I sincerely hope that the recipes in the book will inspire you to try new things and add some excitement to your meals.

Thank you again for your support and for being a part of this journey with me. I hope my book will bring you many happy and delicious moments in the kitchen.

www.ingramcontent.com/pod-product-compliance
Lightning Source LLC
Chambersburg PA
CBHW051319110526
44590CB00031B/4403